VIKINGS

LONGSHIPS AND BATTLE-AXES

Written by Rosemary Border

Illustrated by Peter Rutherford and Peter Wilks

HENDERSON
PUBLISHING PLC

If you haven't found history much fun so far, it's probably because you got bogged down in the boring bits. History is like a kipper - you sometimes have to work hard to get at the tasty bits. Our old history master, Mr Salmon - inevitably nicknamed Old Fishface - was a good historian. He also knew a lot about kids; and that was what made him a good teacher. At the start of a lesson Old Fishface handed out fact sheets.

"If you learn this by heart you'll know enough about the Vikings" (or castles, or Greeks, or whatever) "to pass your exams. Now I'll tell you something really interesting." And he did. He gave us all the tasty bits.
Sometimes we were so spellbound by his tales that we didn't even hear the bell at the end of the lesson. I have forgotten almost everything in Old Fishface's fact sheets, but not his stories. I keep them in a compartment of my mind labelled Useless Information. Sticky History is real history with all the boring bits taken out. (I didn't make any of it up, honestly!) A sort of fillet of history - no skin, no bones, just the tasty bits.

Rosemary Border 1995

WHO WERE THE VIKINGS?
(and what's a vik?)

The Vikings came from Scandinavia (that's Norway, Sweden and Denmark in case you didn't know). Most experts think the Vikings got their name from *vik*, which means fjord, the deep, narrow kind of bay you find in Norway.

So why did the Vikings have a bad reputation? Possibly because they didn't have enough good farming land of their own, so they grabbed other people's. But this is only part of the story. The Vikings liked fighting and adventure. Their motto could be "Have sword (and bad attitude problem), will travel".

> ### USELESS INFORMATION - DO YOU UNDERSTAND ME?
>
> Wherever they went, the Vikings learned the language and customs of the people there. The Vikings' own languages are still spoken in Norway, Sweden and Denmark. These languages are so like each other that if a Sweden speaks slowly, a Norwegian can understand him.

You have to remember that the Vikings themselves haven't left much information about their raiding trips. Most of what we know about them comes from the victims, especially the monks whose monasteries got burned and looted. They were so scared of the threats, they used to pray, "Dear God, save us from the Northmen." Obviously, they didn't say too much about the Vikings who stayed quietly at home, farming and fishing and making pots.

THE VIKINGS' WORLD

This map shows the parts of the world which the Vikings explored and invaded. Of course, many Vikings stayed at home in Scandinavia. But there was not enough space there for everyone. Suppose a farmer had three sons. The oldest son would get the farm after his father's death, but there would be nowt for t'other two, so they had to leave home. Some sailed west and settled in Britain and Ireland. Some sailed south and raided Normandy, where they settled and became the Normans. William the Conqueror, who invaded Britain in 1066, was a Viking.

"And Bjorn brought me this from his last trip."

4

Some Vikings did venture south in search of sun and sand; they are known to have raided and traded in North Africa. Some sailed thousands of miles east, along the great rivers of Russia (*although it wasn't called Russia back then*). Many settled there. Some reached Constantinople and fought for the Emperor. Some sailed north, first to Iceland, where thousands of Vikings made their homes, then to Greenland. And a few adventurous Vikings reached America hundreds of years before Christopher Columbus, who took all the credit.

The Vikings traded with people all over the place. They met Arab traders on their way back from China with long caravans of camels, and bought silk and spices from them. Their own home-made drinks were beer (made from barley) and mead (made from honey), but they brought home wine from Greece, France and eastern Europe. Archaeologists digging up Viking settlements have found things which were made thousands of miles from Scandinavia. They show how far the Vikings travelled.

USELESS INFORMATION - DOWN ON THE BY!

Wherever they settled, the Vikings left their own place names. York in the north of England was once a Viking settlement called Jorvik. Many of York's streets are called gate, which means a street in 'Viking'. English place names like Whitby (a by was a farm), Thwaite (a thwaite was a meadow) and Thorpe (a thorpe was a village), are pure Viking.

THE STORY OF THE VIKINGS

Old Fishface would have given you a fact sheet on this, but this is much more fun.

The Vikings had probably been raiding for years, but the first we know of them is when they raided the monastery of Lindisfarne on the north-east coast of Britain in 793 AD. In the next few years the Vikings raided Ireland, too. Some settled on the Scottish islands and on the Isle of Man. Meanwhile other bands of Vikings were raiding the coasts of France, Germany, Spain and Italy and even north Africa. They killed, they looted and they took slaves.

Adventurous Vikings sailed their dragon ships down the big rivers of eastern Europe. When they ran out of river, they picked up their ships and carried them. Well, to be more exact, they rolled them over rows of tree trunks. Many settled in what is now Russia. Some Vikings settled in Constantinople, where they signed up for the Emperor's bodyguard.

In 830 AD a Christian monk went to Sweden to try to persuade the Vikings to become Christians, but it was 100 years before they did. Even after Christianity was the official religion, many Vikings carried on worshipping their old gods. Meanwhile, the Vikings were raiding England and Ireland more than ever before. Some camped there during the winter, then went raiding again in the spring. Eventually, many stopped raiding and made their homes in England and Ireland.

7

Meanwhile many Vikings were looking for new places to raid and to settle. In 860 they found Iceland (*not that it was ever lost, but the Vikings didn't know it was there yet*). By 930 about 10,000 Vikings had settled there.

In 867 AD, Viking raiders from Denmark captured York, and from then on it was down hill for the Brits. Soon Vikings had settled all over the north east of England. After years of fighting, the English king agreed to share the country between the English and the Danes. The Danish part was called the Danelaw and many Vikings settled there peacefully with their families. The agreement did not stop more Vikings from raiding, however. The English paid them money to keep away. Then, in 1016, Canute, the Danish king, invaded England and a Viking became king of England.

In 911 AD, a Viking called Rollo raided the northern coast of what is now France. The local king agreed to give him some land in exchange for peace. The Vikings called this land Normandy. It was these people who in 1066 invaded England. William the Conqueror, a Viking, beat Harold, another Viking, at Hastings and became king of England and Normandy.

USELESS INFORMATION - AFTER THE BATTLE

When Norman knights went into battle, they wore costumes of chainmail to protect them. When the fighting was over, they were said to look like porcupines, due to all the enemy arrows stuck in the metal links!

8

Meanwhile, in Iceland, a Viking called Eric the Red (named for his hair and football allegiances) heard about an island which nobody had explored. In 982 he set sail and found a huge island which he called Greenland. For most of the year Greenland was not at all green, but Eric thought a little white lie about the name would make people want to live there. He went home and spread the news, and many Vikings sailed to Greenland to settle.

In 1002 AD, Eric's son Leif sailed west from Greenland and found land. Experts think he reached Labrador or Newfoundland in Canada. He came home and told wonderful tales about the grapes he saw growing there, and he called the land Vinland (not the same as Finland). Some Vikings followed Leif there. Well, it sounds better than Greenland which isn't green, doesn't it!

THE VIKINGS AT HOME

A Viking farm was hardly worthy of the name, as there is not much farming to be done. It is a beautiful place with mountains, forests and lakes, but not very fertile. Not much use at all, really.

This is the loo - a seat over a deep hole. For privacy, it has a hut built around it. Everyone who 'spends a penny' shovels some earth into the hole. When it is full the slaves dig a new hole and put the hut on top of that.

The hut is often found in the nettles at the back of the house. So it's ouch if you crouch!

An important man and his family live in this house, helped by their 'freemen'. It's a bit of a joke, really, calling them 'free' men. They don't own any land, and work only for the richer men - but at least they are better off than the slaves, who live in a hut near the main house. The freemen live in their own houses nearby. Their wives and children work on the farm, too.

The floor of the living quarters would need cleaning regularly. It would be covered in the day-to-day mess the family made - you know, animal bones, shellfish shells, feathers, fur from last night's supper...no vacuum cleaners either, remember? Basketloads of bones, eggshells and rotten vegetables would be left out for the binmen every week. (*Joke - actually, they were tipped into the back yards every now and then - hygenic? I don't think so.*)

Food is kept here. There isn't enough room in the main house. Viking refrigerators were non-existent, so the food had to be salted and smoked to keep it 'fresh' - probably not what you would expect from fresh produce today, but edible at least.

The slaves live in the scabby little place on the left. They were all captured during raids, and are made to do the dirtiest work. They have iron collars round their necks, so that everyone can see they are slaves. The fact that they are doing the rotten jobs is a bit of a clue, too!

The big hut is used for keeping carts (*for summer*), sledges (*for winter*) and farm and fishing equipment safe and dry.

This stone is called soapstone. It is no use for building, but in the winter the Vikings carve it into beautiful bowls, lamps and ornaments. They trade these for things they need.

11

INSIDE THE LONGHOUSE

Only the chief and his wife have a bed. The other members of the family sleep on platforms with furs and blankets to keep them warm. The slaves sleep on the floor with the dogs (a sort of living-duvet).

Cupboards haven't been invented yet. Everyone keeps their belongings in wooden chests. The most valuable things are kept in a chest with strong iron hinges and a lock.

Most cloth is home-made by the women in the house, but the Vikings sometimes buy silk and cotton from Eastern traders.

Viking bread is made at home - there are no specialist bakers. It is difficult to chew and very hard on the teeth. As the corn is ground, bits of stone from the grinder get into the flour and end up in the loaves! And there are no dentists - if you have toothache, it means either putting up with the pain or having your tooth pulled out!

here is no glass in the windows.
e Vikings know about glass, but
t for windows. They have
ooden shutters to keep out the
ld - but they keep out the light
o! So on winter days you have to
oose between light or warmth.

here's no oven in the house - everything is cooked
the open fire. There's no chimney ; the smoke is
pposed to find its way out through a hole in the roof.
t night, the only light comes from the fire and from
all oil lamps. The lamps give out a very poor light,
d they make a lot of smoke and smell nasty.

**USELESS INFORMATION -
IRONING WITHOUT IRONS**

The Vikings ironed their clothes
with big heavy lumps of glass,
which they heated on the fire.

People sit at the table on long wooden
benches. Only the chief has a chair.

VIKING SHIPS

The Vikings are most famous for their longships. Another name for these is dragon ships. At sea, every longship had a carved dragon on the prow (*the front*). There was often an eye carved on the prow, so the ship 'could see where it was going'. In port, the Vikings removed the dragons in case they attracted evil spirits.

D.I.Y. BUILDING A LONGSHIP

Take the trunk of a very tall oak tree. Shape it to make the keel of the ship. Join curved pieces at the back and front to make the stern and bow of the ship.

Now cut long planks from pine trees. Lay them so they overlap one another. (Ships which are built in this way are said to be clinker-built). Fasten them together with iron rivets. Put wool soaked in tar between the planks so the joints don't let in water.

Put the ribs and cross-beams inside the ship. You need a big, heavy block c wood at the bottom of the ship to hold the mast.

"Oh, this sounds easy."

"It's one of those new-fangled anti-theft dragons. You simply lift it off and lock it into the cargo hold."

The Viking longships were long and sleek and very fast. The Vikings could row them along quite shallow rivers. They did not depend on the wind, because they had oars as well as a sail. When the Vikings fought at sea, they lowered the sail and stored it on a special trestle, and used the deck as a fighting platform. The smallest longships had 26 oars, 13 on each side. Some longships had as many as 70 oars, 35 on each side.

Now build the deck of the ship. Don't nail down all the floorboards. You will need to get inside to bail water out of the bottom of the ship in stormy weather. Also, you will want to store spare oars and other gear there.

Fit the big steering oar at the stern, on the right hand (starboard) side.

Make holes in the ship's sides for the oars. Each hole needs a wooden disc to cover it to keep the water out.

"Now, I know why they call it starboard."

USELESS INFORMATION - STARBOARD

All Viking ships had a big steering oar at the back right-hand side of the ship. Sailors call that side the starboard side, from the Viking word styra, to steer.

15

LET'S RAID!

Imagine getting ready to go on holiday - with 40 men, who have to pack their weapons, enough food for a long voyage, and all the spare ropes, sails and so on that you could possibly need. That's how organised the Vikings had to be when setting off on a raid.

Work had to continue on the farm while they were away - the animals had to be cared for, the crops had to be tended and the everyday work had to go on. But the men spent every spare minute getting their ship, their weapons and themselves fit to fight.

HOT WORK!

In his workshop the smith counts the swords and spears, helmets and shields, bows and battleaxes and checks each one. His apprentice works hard with his bellows until the charcoal glows hot. The iron has to be red hot before the smith can work it. When it is ready, he takes an iron bar in his tongs and beats it into shape on his anvil. He is making an axe head.

USELESS INFORMATION -

What has wings and horns and sits on your head?
Answer - your helmet. Vikings hoped that the decorated helmets would make them look more fearful to their enemies.
Some helmets had wings - the wearers hoped to be as swift as birds.
The helmets with horns were supposed to make their owners as strong and brave as bulls.

"Don't forget your helmet, lovey."

Fit to Fight

The men are training, like footballers before the big match. Even the youngest boys learn to fight. They wrestle and box, and they learn to handle swords, axes and spears and to shoot with bows and arrows.

Today the boys are watching and learning while the grown-ups practise with their weapons. They throw their spears at straw targets. They thrust their spears into dummies stuffed with sand or straw. They practise shooting their arrows at small targets hanging on strings from the trees. It is useful to be able to hit a moving target - enemies don't stand still and wait to be shot at!

Loading the Ship

Everybody helps to load the ship. Here are some of the things the Vikings will need on their raid:

- Chests for everyone's personal belongings. The Vikings also sat on their chests (eh?) when they were rowing the ship.

- The chief's tent and bed (guess where the others slept!)

- Sleeping bags made of animal skins

- Weapons
- Food - especially dried meat and fish, also sour milk (like yogurt, but without the sugar). The Vikings hope to steal more interesting food on their first raid.

- Fresh water

"But, dear this is Tupperware. It *will* keep."

AND THEY'RE OFF!

At last all the gear is stowed. It is time to launch the ship. This is done on a slipway of logs. Freemen and slaves push the ship over the logs. At dawn the dragon ship glides down the fjord towards the open sea. The mast is down and the ship is pulled along by just her oars. The women and children wave goodbye. Will they ever see their men again? Some may be killed in battle or drowned at sea.

The men are excited to be off raiding again after the long, boring winter, but the fun won't start for a while yet. They face several days and nights on board ship with very little to do except row, eat and sleep and watch the waves. Space is very cramped. There are no books to read - the Vikings do not go in for reading.

When they get out to sea they raise the mast and hoist the sail. This is not as easy as it sounds - the mast weighs about 300 kilos and there are no cranes to move it. Up goes the sail. The crew use ropes to move the big square sail to catch the wind.

Meanwhile in the nearby fjords other ships are setting out. The Vikings prefer to travel in groups of longships.

Get Lost! (Not very likely...)

The Vikings used sunstones to help them find their way. A sunstone is a piece of glass-like rock called Iceland spar. It becomes opaque when it is pointed towards the sun, even on a cloudy day.

They also had very simple devices for sighting the sun and stars; nobody is sure how they worked, but the Vikings probably held them up to check the ship's direction against the sun or stars.

The ship had a windvane to show which way the wind is blowing. The Vikings knew a lot about the wind and weather. They also watched animals and birds for clues about weather conditions and where land was likely to be found.

USELESS INFORMATION - TWO IN A BAG

The Vikings slept on deck, out in the open, in two-man sleeping bags made of animal skins. It made sense to share a sleeping bag to keep warm.

RAIDING A MONASTERY

The Vikings soon learned that ordinary villages were not worth raiding. Most of the villagers were very poor; there might be a few slaves to be had, but no treasure and very little food. The best place to raid was a monastery. There were plenty of those along the coast of Ireland and north east England. Some were burned and looted several times in not very many years.

The raiders were looking for three things: treasure, food and slaves. They had to act fast, before news of their raid could bring armed men to defend the monastery. They organised themselves into groups. One group would snatch the treasure from the church while a second group set fire to the other buildings to force the people out of them. Then they would kill anyone who put up a fight and take the rest prisoner. The third group went out to the fields and slaughtered any sheep and cattle they could find.

This was a "hit and run" raid. The Vikings did not hang about - they loaded their loot into the longship and sailed a few miles down the coast. There they barbecued a sheep on the beach, checked their weapons, bandaged each other's wounds and rallied round for another raid.

FAME AT LAST

After an especially successful or eventful raid, the Vikings would tell their story to the folks at home and a professional storyteller might make a saga or even compose a song about it.

More importantly, their friends would know where the richest pickings were to be found. They would give a monastery a few years to rebuild and collect some more treasure, then go and do it over again.

"Have you seen any burning monasteries?"

"Sorry, No"

"Have you seen any burning monasteries?"

"I wonder where the lads are?"

"No"

21

For the monks and the people on the nearby farms, the Viking raid felt like the end of the world. A young monk called Dominic, who escaped being taken prisoner by hiding behind a rubbish dump, tells his story. Dominic is imaginary, but several monks like him did write down their stories. A few of these survived Viking raids and are in museums today.

DOMINIC'S STORY

"I was in the school house practising my writing when the church bell started to ring. That meant danger! We all rushed out to see what was happening. Many axemen, howling like devils from Hell, were hacking at our gates. With a splintering crash, the gates gave way and in poured Northmen in gull-wing helmets, waving swords and axes and thrusting fiercely with spears. I dived behind the rubbish dump and covered my ears to drown the noise.

The Abbot sent our fastest runner, Brother Anselm, to the village to fetch help. Then he picked up the cross from the church and walked calmly towards the raiders, holding the cross up high. "Peace to you, brothers," he said. Their leader snatched the cross - and stabbed our Abbot through the heart! Then the Northmen began their deadly work. Some surged into the church to look for treasure. With my own eyes I saw a big ugly Northman coming out with our Holy Book and a silver cup. Another came out with his arms full of books. He tore their jewelled covers off and stuffed them into a bag. Then he threw the pages away. I cried bitterly as I saw the precious Word of God blowing in the wind and trailing in the mud. After the Northmen had gone, I picked up the pages. Perhaps one day we can bind the book again; but the Northmen burned many more.

rmed men came from the village, but they were no match for the Northmen. Some of the aiders herded our sheep and cattle off to their ship. Others set fire to the thatched roofs of he houses in the village. When the people came out, the Northmen attacked them. Much ater, when all was quiet, I crept out of my hiding place…"

PROTECTION MONEY

he governments of the day tried fighting the Vikings, but they could not guard every bit f coast, there were just not enough men. Some kings tried paying them to stay away, but hat did not work either. The Vikings accepted the silver and gold happily, then sailed ome and told their friends. Soon more and more longships would land, greedy for free andouts.

Vegetarians? Not Likely...

After a good summer's raiding, the longships sailed home, packed tight with goods and prisoners. The people gave their men a fine welcome and prepared a mighty feast. They slaughtered cows and sheep and speared deer and wild boar in the forest. They baked bread and picked vegetables from the garden. They opened barrels of stolen French wine and home brewed beer. The cooking went on in the middle of the hall, on a huge fire inside four low stone walls. Great iron pots of stew hung over the fire. Here is the menu:

Roast Beef

Baked Beef

Beef Stew

Roast Mutton

Roast Wild Boar

Roast Venison (deer)

Boiled Pork

Braised Wild Boar Steaks

Cabbage

Peas

Bread

Honey Cakes

To drink:

Home-brewed beer

Mead, made from honey

Juices of wild fruits

Milk

The Vikings ate a lot of their food with their fingers. They had spoons, made from metal, wood or horn, for sloppy foods like stew.

To be fair to the flesh-eating Vikings, we should point out that their land was not ideal for growing vegetables.

Some meat for general consumption was bought from traders and markets. Often, the food displayed would be covered in swarms of flies. No problem though - these quickly flew off in great clouds when the meat was lifted up and carried away.

"That'll teach you to bolt your food."

In the Autumn, domestic animals were slaughtered to provide the meat for the winter. As the cattle were brought into town from the countryside, the streets became slippery with cowpats.

How to Cook Meat

Spit Roasting

No, you don't spit on it! A spit is a long stick which you poke through the joint of meat (or the whole animal). You stand the spit on a trestle over a fire and get a slave to keep turning the spit so the meat cooks evenly. You can sprinkle herbs and salt over the meat as it cooks. Yum.

Boiling

Dig a square hole and line it with wood. Fill the hole with water. Put some pieces of meat in the water, with salt, herbs, juniper berries and mustard seeds. Now get a slave to put hot stones from the fire into the hole to heat the water. Mind the steam!

Baking

The Vikings made a big hole in the ground and filled it with stones which had been heated in a fire. They laid the meat on top, packed in more hot stones and covered the whole lot with earth until the meat was cooked.

Useless Information - Drinking Horns

The Vikings used cups, but they also drank from the horns of cattle. The big problem (or advantage, depending how you looked at it) was that you couldn't put your half-drunk horn down without it tipping over and spilling. So you had to drink it all up at one go - shame!

25

TELL US ANOTHER ONE, DO

At their feasts the Vikings loved to listen to songs and stories. Travelling musicians and storytellers went from hall to hall - sort of New Age Vikings. They performed old songs and stories, and sometimes made up new ones about the adventures of whoever was giving them a free feast. They had to keep all their tales and tunes in their heads, because there were no books (or tape recorders).

The Vikings, frankly, were not very cultured. For Christian monks like Dominic, reading and writing were part of their way of life. Some of their writing has survived; it tells us a great deal about them and about the Vikings. The Vikings themselves did not write about their adventures. They did not use writing for everyday things like stories or letters. They had no storybooks. The Vikings passed their tales on by word of mouth. They told stories about gods and heroes and adventurers. These stories are called sagas. Hundreds of years later, when more people could read and write, they wrote down their stories.

GWUESOME GRAFFITI

Viking letters are called runes. They are made up of straight lines to make them easier to carve into stone and wood. (Have you ever tried carving SP loves CB onto a tree trunk? I should jolly well hope not...) The Vikings carved runes on tombstones to say who was buried there, and on their possessions to show who the things belonged to. When the Vikings became Christian, they learned the ABC which we use today.

"Oh, me runes are in ruins!"

Not many Vikings learned to read and write. They left it to the experts. Writing was done by runemasters, just as ironwork was done by smiths.

Children did not learn to read and write. Instead they learned the things they needed to know - farming, fishing, fighting, weaving, cooking - from their parents and the freemen and women around them.

F	U	TH	A	R	K	H	N
I	A	S	T	B	M	L	R

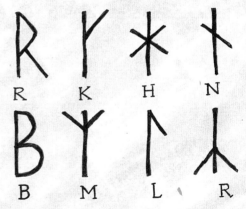

HURRAH!
As far as we can tell from excavations and documentation, there were no Viking schools.

F U TH A R K

THE VIKING 'BIG BANG' THEORY

In the beginning was Ginnungagap, the Big Nothing. In the north was Niflheim, all darkness and ice and freezing fog; and in the south was Muspell, all fire-spouting volcanoes and choking gases. Where the two met, the ice of Niflheim melted; and out of the water drops came a terrible giant called Ymir. At the same time, a monstrous cow came out of the ice. From her udders flowed four great rivers of milk. While Ymir drank his fill and grew strong, the cow licked the blocks of ice. As the ice melted under her warm tongue, a head appeared, then a body. This was Buri, the father of the Gods.

"and then the cow licked the ice and a body came out of it..."

CARVING UP YMIR

Buri had three sons, Odin, the chief of the gods, and his two brothers. Together the three killed Ymir, and from his body they made the world. They made the soil from his flesh, and the mountains from his bones. And from the giant's blood they made the seas and lakes. His teeth became the rocks and stony places, and his hair became the grass and trees. From the dome of Ymir's skull the brothers made the sky, and they threw his brains up into the sky to make the clouds. (*They probably made the motorways from his shoelaces later in history.*)

NORTH, SOUTH, EAST AND WEST

Meanwhile, maggots bred inside Ymir's corpse (*yum*). They became the dwarves, and the gods gave them the hills and rocks and caves for their home. Four dwarves, called North, South, East and West, held up the four corners of the sky. They were quite tall, for dwarves. Meanwhile, the glowing sparks that flew up from Muspell's fiery volcanoes became the stars. Two beautiful children called Sun and Moon raced across the sky. Behind each of them panted a terrible, hungry wolf. ("*One day,*" said the Viking storyteller grimly, "*the wolves will catch them and eat them…*")

THE FIRST MAN AND WOMAN

One day Odin and his brothers were walking by the seashore when they found two pieces of driftwood. They took out their knives and carved the driftwood into a man and a woman. Then the gods gave them life and understanding.

The Vikings believed that the world was divided into three parts. Niflheim (or, in some sagas, Hel) was the underworld. Midgard was Middle-earth, the home of men and women. Asgard was the home of the gods. A mighty tree called Yggdrasil, the World tree, held them together. An eagle perched in its tallest branches and a serpent gnawed at the roots. The eagle and the serpent were always quarrelling, and a squirrel ran up and down the tree trunk playing one off against the other. The Vikings believed that Yggdrasil was rotting away, and that when it fell apart the world would end.

VIKING HEAVEN

The Vikings were not afraid of dying in battle. They believed that the Valkyries, Odin's warrior handmaidens, would take them straight to Asgard to live in Odin's great hall, Valholl, the Hall of the Slain. There the heroes spent all day fighting. At the end of the day their wounds were magically healed, and they all sat down to feast on roast meat and drink mead and beer. Those Valkyries who were not out collecting more heroes hovered by the tables, keeping everyone's drinking-horns filled, while Odin watched, fondling his two pet wolves. After a good night's sleep, the warriors were ready for another day of feasting and fighting.

Valholl, then, was the Viking heaven, a non-stop feast of food and fighting and female company. Most people nowadays would get very tired of it (or maybe not), but to the Vikings Valholl was perfect in every way. After all life was hard then, and pleasures were simple and few.

DOCTOR, DOCTOR

Dying in battle was all very well, but nobody wanted to die until it was really necessary (*oh, really?*). The Viking doctors knew a lot about wounds and broken bones (*they got plenty of practice treating those!*), and a little about diseases. They made medicines and ointments from herbs. Mostly the sick person died, or got better, in spite of the doctors. Meanwhile the sick person's family would pray to the gods to step in if the doctor could not help.

USELESS INFORMATION -
THOR'S HAMMER

Every Viking warrior wore a lucky charm called an amulet, in the shape of a hammer, around his neck. This was Mjollnir, the mighty stone hammer of the thunder god Thor. Mjollnir means lightning. Warriors prayed to Thor to help them to fight and die bravely.

THE VIKING WAY OF DEATH

When someone died, how the body was disposed of depended on how rich and important the person was. A rich man might be laid in a grave lined with planks of wood, with his weapons, a chest containing his belongings, a joint of beef and a barrel of beer. Sometimes dogs, horses and even slaves were killed to be buried with their master. Oh, how cosy!

Poor people were buried in graves with a few things beside them. A poor woman might be buried with a comb, a cheap brooch, a barrel of milk in case she needed a drink and her spindle in case she felt like a spot of spinning in the next world.
A woman's work is never done…

Sometimes the Vikings burned their dead warriors on a funeral pyre, a sort of bonfire of wood. Before putting the body on the pyre, the dead man's sword was bent and his shield and spear were broken in two. Then they were thrown on the pyre.

"DUST TO DUST... AND SHIPS TO EARTH?"

Some rich and important people were buried in ships with all their belongings. The Vikings thought the dead person would sail away to the next world. Ships like these have been found at Okstand and Oseberg in Norway and at Sutton Hoo in Suffolk. The Okstad ship was a real longboat, lean and fast with holes for 16 pairs of oars. The ship at Oseberg was more like a royal barge than a longship. It belonged to a Viking queen. Here are just a few of the things that were buried with her:

Jewellery, a beautifully carved wooden cart, sledges, beds, tapestries, weaving looms, barrels, cooking gear, a bucket, harness for horses, shoes, personal belongings such as combs...

...and an ox and a slave girl.

Page 8

Page 16

Page 19

Page 8

Page 17

Page 14

Page 9

Page 19

Page 17

Page 36

Page 18

Page 30

Page 17

Page 37

Page 31

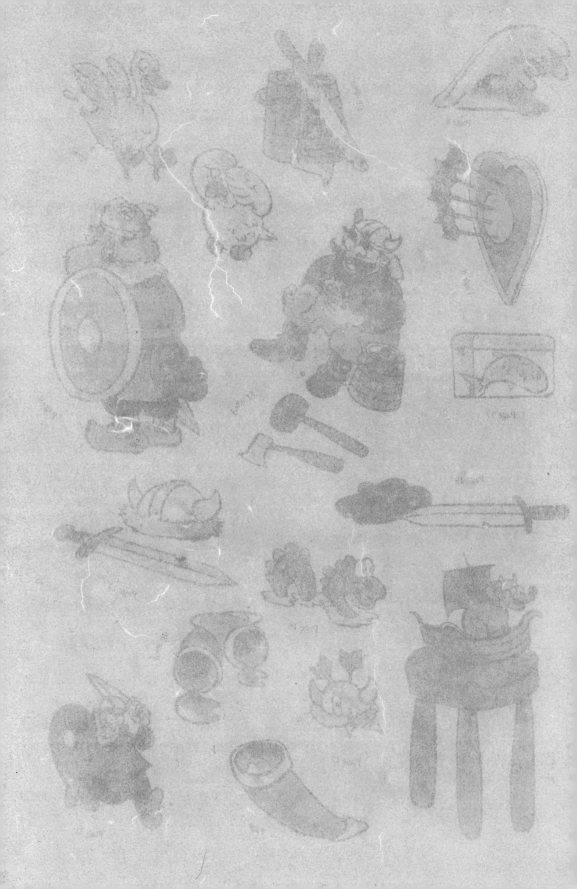

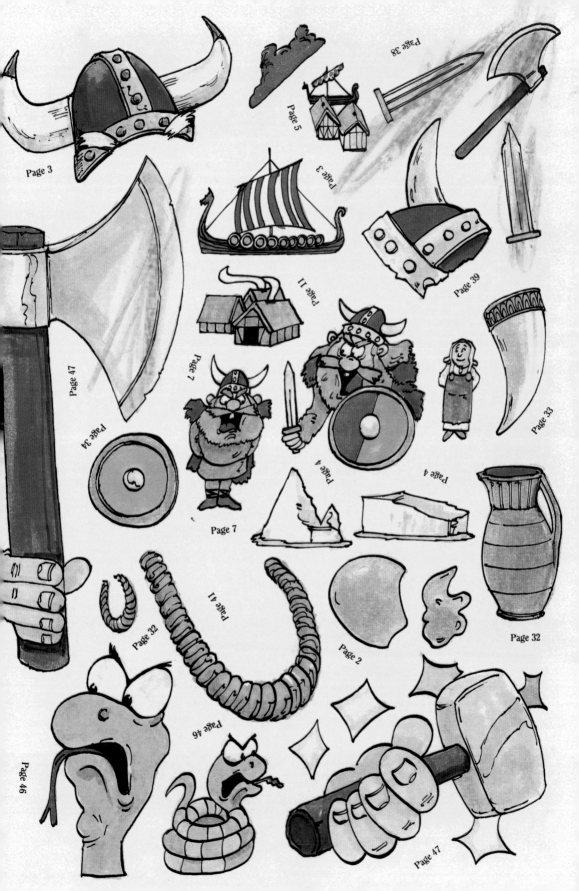

Page 12

Page 12

Page 12

Page 12

Page 11

Page 12

Page 11

Page 11

Page 11

Page 11

Page 47

Page 11

Page 12

Page 44

Page 12

Page 21

Page 21

Page 23

Page 20

Page 29

Page 24

Page 24

Page 35

Page 35

Page 24

Page 42

Page 12

The Sutton Hoo ship rotted away, leaving just the metal parts and the outline of the ship with the treasures inside. But the clay in which the Okstad and Oseberg ships were buried preserved them. You can see the ships in a beautiful, specially built museum at Oslo in Norway. From them we have learnt almost all we know about how the Vikings built their ships.

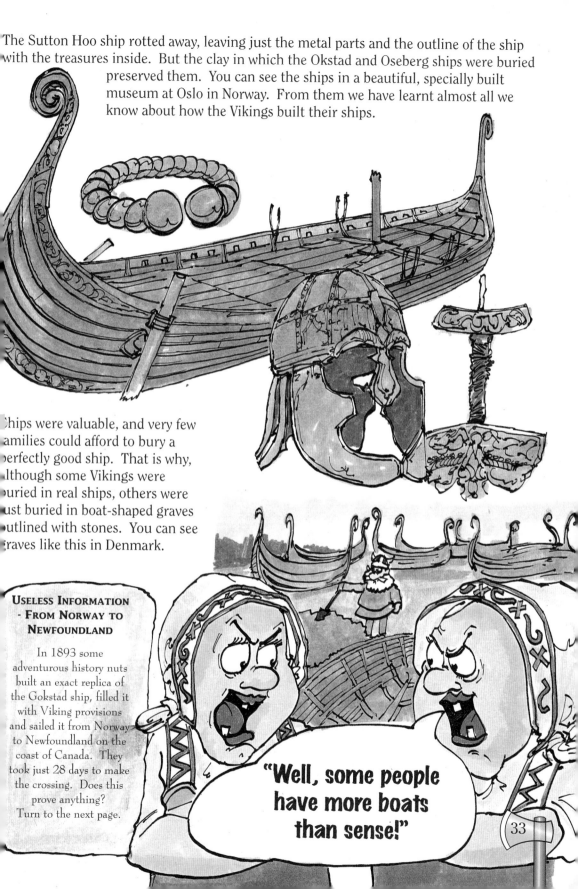

Ships were valuable, and very few families could afford to bury a perfectly good ship. That is why, although some Vikings were buried in real ships, others were just buried in boat-shaped graves outlined with stones. You can see graves like this in Denmark.

USELESS INFORMATION - FROM NORWAY TO NEWFOUNDLAND

In 1893 some adventurous history nuts built an exact replica of the Gokstad ship, filled it with Viking provisions and sailed it from Norway to Newfoundland on the coast of Canada. They took just 28 days to make the crossing. Does this prove anything? Turn to the next page.

"Well, some people have more boats than sense!"

33

Viking Explorers

The Vikings reached the New World long before Christopher Columbus, who got all the glory. But they didn't suddenly say, "Let's go and look for America," and sail into the sunset. The people who recreated the journey from Norway to Newfoundland were brave and adventurous, but they did not know much about how the Vikings reached the New World.

To start with, the Vikings took the scenic route! First they explored the Shetland Islands to the far north of Shetland. Many settled there and lived quietly (*by Viking standards*), farming and fishing. As early as 700 AD they reached the Faroe islands and settled there.

Next stop Iceland. By about 930 AD, the Vikings had settled on all the usable land there and many of them were looking around for more places to explore. Eric the Red was one of these.

Eric in Trouble

Eric got his name from his fiery red hair. He seems to have had a fiery temper too, because he had to leave Norway in a hurry as he'd killed someone. He sailed to Iceland, where he married a lady called Thjodhild, but very soon he was in trouble again. He got into a fight and killed two men. In 982 the local Thing (*see page 42*) made him an outlaw.

The New Land

Eric and his men set sail - and found an island. The place where they first landed was pretty bleak, but they sailed further south and found fjords and forests, rather like Norway. When Eric reckoned that everyone in Iceland had forgotten about his spot of bother, he sailed back there and tried to persuade people to settle on the new island. He called it Greenland, which sounded very inviting. 25 ships set out with him in 986 but only 14 reached Greenland. Some were shipwrecked, and others lost their nerve and sailed back to Iceland.

"Honest, it's from Greenland."

THE GREEN LAND -
JUST AN ADVERTISING GIMMICK?

Eric wasn't really lying when he named his new land. The southern tip of Greenland is actually no further north than the Shetland Islands, and further south than Iceland. The settlers were able to farm the land. Eric built a house for him and Thjodhild. It was made of stone and turf, and they called it Brattahlid. Eric and Thjodhild had three sons, Leif, Thorvald and Thorstein, and a daughter called Freydis. Altogether, the Viking settlers built 280 farms over the next 50 years or so. The Vikings did not realise at first that someone else had arrived before them - the Inuit or Eskimos. But they lived much further north, and for a long time there was plenty of room for everyone.

The Vikings farmed, they hunted walrus, reindeer, arctic foxes and polar bear and traded the furs and tusks for things they needed from home, such as timber for shipbuilding, and metal for weapons. They formed their own government and made their own laws. In 1000, Christianity came to Greenland. Eric - typically - was dead against it, according to the sagas. But Thjodhild was converted, and she built a little church at Brattahlid, some way away from the farm so as not to hurt Eric's feelings. Eric died in 1001. He probably did not want a Christian burial.

BJARNI GETS LOST

One of the Vikings who sailed to Greenland with Eric the Red was Herjolf Bardarson. He built a farm there called Herjolfness. Herjolf had a son called Bjarni, who did not manage to set off at the same time as the other settlers. On Bjarni's journey he ran into foul weather, with howling gales and swirling fog - and got lost. When the weather improved a little, Bjarni saw hills and forest to the south west. Eric had described Greenland and Bjarni had a fair idea what he was looking for (*although if he was looking for some green land he was in trouble already*). He realised that he had sailed too far off course. So he sailed north and sighted land again. Nope, this couldn't be Greenland either - too many trees, too flat, not green either. Four days later, the wind blew up again and actually carried his ship to Herjolfness (*whee!!*), where he met his father and told him all about his adventures. Then, very sensibly, Bjarni sold his ship, settled down and farmed and fished at Herjolfness. The lands he had seen were just something to talk about on a cold winter evening by the fire. Zzzz...

"... so then we packed up and set sail for some more green bits..."

36

Leif the Lucky

Leif, the son of Eric the Red, was the man who bought Bjarni's ship. He wanted to find the places Bjarni had seen. Leif sailed south west, and came to a land of ice and rock which he called Helluland ("*Slabland*"). He sailed on and found a low-lying coast with forests, which he called Markland ("*Forestland*"). He sailed further south, and reached a beautiful coast. The weather was mild, there was grass for cattle, the rivers were full of leaping salmon and grapes were growing wild. So they called this land Vinland ("*Wineland*"). They spent the winter there, and in the spring they sailed home to Greenland.

As they approached Greenland, Leif and his men rescued 15 people from a ship which had been wrecked on a reef. It was this adventure, not his trip to Vinland, which earned Leif the Lucky his nickname.

Where was Vinland?

Experts think Helluland was Baffin Island and Markland was the southern coast of Labrador (*they're on modern maps if you can be bothered to find an atlas*). The real problem is Vinland. Nobody is sure how long Leif sailed before sighting this land of plenty. Did he reach Newfoundland? Did he get even farther south? Will we ever know?

USELESS INFORMATION - WINE OR GRASS?
Some experts say that Vinland does not mean "Wineland" at all, but "Grassland". Vin means both wine and grass in Old Norse. We may never know.

37

THE ONE THAT GOT AWAY

Leif's brother Thorvald was deeply interested in Vinland. He gathered a crew of 30 and set off for Vinland. They found the place where Leif had spent the winter, and they spent the winter there, too. (*Copycats.*)

At first they thought Vinland was quite uninhabited. Then they found three skin boats on the beach. Three men were hiding under each boat, and they rushed out and attacked the Vikings. The Vikings killed eight, but the ninth got away and fetched his friends. While Thorvald and his men were asleep, a crowd of the strangers, whom the Vikings called Skraelings ("*wretched people*"), attacked, and Thorvald was killed. His men buried him in Vinland, and in the spring sailed home to tell Thorvald's family.

YET *ANOTHER* EXPEDITION

Meanwhile, Thorstein, Eric's third son, had died and a Viking from Norway called Thorfinn had married his widow, Gudrid (short for 'good riddance to Thorstein', possibly). Thorfinn and Gudrid set out for Vinland with 60 men and women. They took farm animals, too, including a bull; they can't have had an easy journey…(*must have been pretty niffy for a start*).

They found Leif's houses and spent a peaceful winter. Then, next summer, a big band of Skraelings (*those wretched people again*) came out of the woods. But the bull bellowed and pawed the ground, and the Skraelings ran for their lives. It was obviously worth putting up with the bull on the boat.

Eventually, the Vikings and the Skraelings started trading. The Vikings exchanged milk from their cows for furs and cloth. But they did not trust the Skraelings; so they built a stout wooden fence round their houses. There Gudrid gave birth to a son called Snorri - the first non-American ever to be born in America.

The Skraelings became more hostile. Some say the Vikings caught one trying to steal weapons, and killed him. Whatever the reason, the Skraelings and the Vikings became enemies again. At the same time, the Vikings became homesick and eventually the settlers returned to Greenland.

Hang on, you are probably saying. How do you know all this? Thought the Vikings didn't write things down. Well, two sagas, Eric's Saga and the Greenlanders' Saga, have survived. We could just dismiss them as stories, except for one thing…

PROVE IT!

We know for sure that Eric settled at Brattahlid in Greenland, because archaeologists found the ruins. But what about Vinland? Well, in the 1960s archaeologists excavating in Newfoundland uncovered a settlement very like the Viking settlements in Greenland. They could see the foundations of buildings, and they found a few small items, which they realised were Viking. They dated it in the 11th century AD. Was this the place where first Leif and then Thorvald spent the winter, and where the bull scared off the Skraelings?

THE VIKING CLOTHES SHOW

Good evening, everybody, and welcome to the Viking clothes show.

First, we see Astrid, wearing a long, loose dress made of beautifully embroidered silk. Over it she has a pinafore made of two oblongs of linen fastened at the shoulders by two brooches. The linen was grown, spun and woven here in Norway. Arab traders brought the silk by camel from China and her father traded it for furs and jewels.

Notice the beautiful brooches on Astrid's shoulders, stolen from an English nobleman's house. On her feet Astrid is wearing shoes made from soft leather with smart silver buckles. She wears her hair in two long plaits, fastened on top of her head with two beautiful combs made from deer antlers. The combs were made here in Norway, decorated with glass beads from the East.

And now here comes Astrid's boyfriend Sven. He is wearing linen trousers, with a silk tunic on top. Note the beautiful belt made of leather studded with silver. The buckle is fashioned in the shape of a snarling beast. Sven's sword is with the smith being mended, but he is carrying a dagger in a jewelled sheath. Sven brought home the jewels from a gold cup that he - er - found in a monastery in Ireland. On his feet, Sven wears smart deerskin shoes with leather laces called thongs.

Next in our parade we see Olaf the slave boy and his sister Gudrun. They wear whatever they can get hold of. They don't need shoes, their feet are very hard and tough.

Baubles, Bangles and Beads

The Vikings loved jewellery - stolen and home-made. Archaeologists have found Viking ladies buried with wonderful brooches, bracelets, rings and necklaces made of gold and silver and also glass beads from the East. Wealth was easily paraded by wearing ornate cloak-brooches, with beads fastened between them, across their fronts. Jewellery could be made from cheaper metals that looked almost like gold and silver, if you wanted to pretend you were rich. Clever jewellers made convincing fakes from milk-bottle tops and silver foil. (*Just jesting!*)

Useless Information - Useful Antlers!

Deer shed their antlers every year and grow new ones. The Vikings collected the antlers and made beautiful combs from them. They also made spindles, spoons and knife handles.

Useless Information - Comb your Rotten Hair!

Although combs were ornate and often treasured items, they did serve a very practical purpose too. Viking living conditions were ideal for headlice and nits, caught from the dirty houses and bedding. The combs helped a little to clean your head!

41

THE THING

The Vikings meet a few times a year to deal with crimes and make important decisions. This get-together is called 'the Thing'. Only freemen can attend. They come from miles around, and they camp nearby; the Thing can go on for many days. Travelling salesmen and craftsmen come and peddle their wares; a Thing was a cross between Glastonbury festival and the Houses of Parliament (*imagine it if you can!*). In the evenings after the talks, the freemen take part in wrestling or weightlifting.

CRIME AND PUNISHMENT

The Vikings did not send criminals to prison. If a man stole, the Thing ordered his hand to be cut off. Murderers were banished - sent away, like Eric the Red - after paying compensation, called wergild, to the dead man's family. The more important the victim, the greater the wergild. If the murderer did not leave at once, the victim's family were free to kill him, and often did.

USELESS INFORMATION - WATCH THE WITCH

The Vikings were terrified of witches. If a woman was found guilty of witchcraft, she would be either drowned or stoned to death. Executions were a spectator sport; everyone watched the fun.

VIKING WINTERS

The Scandinavian winters are long, cold and dark. Oil for the lamps is scarce, there's nothing good on the TV, so everyone goes to bed very early. Nobody can work on the land, and nobody goes raiding. There's no Christmas, and not even any school holidays to look forward to (no school, you see). The snow lies on the ground for months at a time.

TRICKY TRACKING

In the winter, hungry wolves came out of the forest and tried to carry off the Vikings' farm animals. Then it was time for a wolf hunt. It wasn't exactly difficult to track the wolf, of course, because he left footprints in the snow. The dogs soon cornered him, and the hunters finished him off with their arrows and spears.

FIRESIDE GAMES

In winter the Vikings shut themselves up inside their longhouses and told stories. They also gambled with dice and played board games. Several Viking board games have been found. One is called Hnefetafl - King's Board. Hnefetafl is a war game, like chess. The idea is to surround the other player's king.

Another game is called Halatafl, which is also called Fox and Geese. If the fox jumps over a goose, the goose is killed and has to be taken off the board. The geese can win by crowding the fox so that he can't move.

Another game involves two computer characters beating each other up. One character is a martial arts expert, the other

has a selection of weapons. The more times your character is hit, the more energy you lose (just joking again…).

WINTER FUN

Believe it or not, the Vikings went ice-skating. Their skates were made from bone, and they used short wooden skis for getting about. Nobody is sure if the Vikings went in for skiing for fun, but I bet that one day some inventive boy or girl strapped on a pair of skis, picked up two broom handles and pushed off down the hill…Whee!

Sledges were used for work in the snow instead of carts. In their free moments, everyone liked sledging down a snowy slope. Of course, there were no bin-liners or tea-trays to use as substitutes in those days, you had to have a proper sledge.

A Bedtime Story

The people in the Vikings' stories were very like the Vikings themselves - brave and strong, but also jealous, quarrelsome and cruel. The women in their stories could be as ruthless as the men. Viking stories would, be given an 18 certificate nowadays. I would skip the next few pages if you've just eaten…

The Hoard of Gold

Two brothers, Fafnir and Regin, quarrelled over a hoard of gold. Fafnir changed himself into a dragon and brooded over his treasure in a cave. Regin decided to have his revenge against Fafnir by forging a marvellous sword for a young hero, Sigurd, to get his brother with.

"Dig a pit and attack from underneath," Regin advised. "Fafnir's hide and scales are hard as iron, but his underbelly is as soft as a rabbit's." So Sigurd dug a pit in the track that Fafnir used, and when the dragon came along he thrust his sword deep into Fafnir's soft belly.

The Magic Blood

Now Regin took charge. "Roast Fafnir's heart for me to eat, and drain his blood for me to drink," he ordered. The dragon's heart was magic, anyone who ate it became as brave as any dragon. The blood was (*of course*) magic too. It would give Regin the power to see deep into the hearts of men, and to understand the speech of animals and birds (*how useful?*).

Traitor

Regin, however, received neither of those gifts. While he was roasting the heart Sigurd touched it and burned his finger. He licked his sore finger and tasted the blood. At once he knew what Regin was planning to do. Sigurd drew his sword and slew Regin, and took the golden hoard for himself.

Gudrun and co.

Sigurd went to the kingdom of King Gjuki (*don't ask how you pronounce that*). The king had two sons called Gunnar and Hogni

and a daughter called Gudrun. Sigurd married Gudrun and gave her a ring from his dragon hoard.

Sigurd, Gunnar and Hogni became blood brothers and vowed to help each other at all times. The three heroes went to visit King Atli Gunnar wanted to marry his sister, Brynhild (*bad move*). Brynhild had shut herself up in a tower with a wall of flames in front of it (*a bit drastic, but it gave them the message*).

ORDEAL BY FIRE

"Only the hero who will ride through the flames to win me, shall be my husband," she said.

Gunnar's horse was frightened, so Sigurd disguised himself as Gunnar and rode his own horse through the flames for him (*they were blood brothers, remember*) and won Brynhild. But because he was already married, Sigurd slept beside her with his sword between their two bodies (*what a jolly decent sort of chap*). When they parted in the grey dawn he gave her a ring from the dragon's hoard and she gave him a ring in exchange. Then Gunnar took Brynhild home to Gjuki's kingdom as his wife.

QUARRELLING WIVES

All went well until the two wives fell out.
"My husband's braver than yours," said Gudrun
"He killed a dragon."
"My husband rode through flames to reach me!" retorted Brynhild.
"Oh no he didn't!" said Gudrun. "That was Sigurd. Look - here's the ring you gave him."

Brynhild went straight to her brothers, and told them that she now knew the truth about the hero who rode through the flames to win her. She also told a big fat lie - claiming that Sigurd had made love to her. As you and I know, Sigurd's sword lay between them on the only night they slept together. Brynhild (*sweet, gentle maiden that she was*) urged them to kill him in revenge.

This they did - but with heavy hearts, because it's not very nice, killing your blood brother. To make things worse, they stole his hoard of gold. Then Brynhild killed herself in shame (*serve her right, I say*) and she and Sigurd were burnt on the same funeral pyre. Worra palaver.

AND THERE'S MORE... REVENGE

Gudrun married Brynhild's brother Atli and they had two baby sons. Atli was jealous of his new brothers in law, Gunnar and Hogni (*remember - Sigurd's blood brothers?*) and wanted their hoard for himself. He invited them to a feast. "Don't go - it's a trap!" warned Gudrun. (*She was their sister, remember, and she didn't want them harmed*). But the brothers hid their treasure and went to Atli's house.

Atli grabbed the brothers. He locked Hogni in a cell, then offered Gunnar his life if he would tell him where the treasure was hidden.
"I will," said Gunnar, "if you will bring me my brother's heart." (*What a very nice man.*)
Atli wanted to keep Hogni alive - after all, he was no use to him dead - so he sent his men to kill a slave and bring the heart, still warm and bloody and quivering, on a silver tray.

IT GETS WORSE...

"That's not my brother's heart!" said Gunnar. "Look, it's trembling. Hogni never trembled in his life!"
So Atli brought Hogni in and cut his chest open and tore out his heart - and Hogni laughed in scorn as he died (*peculiar, but they do say Vikings were well 'ard*).
Gunnar laughed too. "Now I know my secret is safe," he said, "for you will never learn about the gold from me!"

Gudrun begged and pleaded with her husband, but Atli threw Gunnar into a pit of poisonous snakes. Gunnar's hands were tied, but he played his harp (where did that come from?) with his feet until at last the snakes' poison reached his heart.

Now Gudrun prepared a terrible revenge on Atli. She killed their two sons and from their skulls she made drinking bowls set in gold and silver. At her brothers' funeral feast she gave Atli the boys' roasted hearts to eat. In the two skull-cups she mixed their blood with mead and gave it to Atli to drink. Then, when he was drunk, she told him what she had done. That night she stabbed Atli and set fire to his house. His entire household perished in the flames.

...Believe it or not, that was <u>not</u> the end of the story. Gudrun married again and there are several more episodes of blood, jealousy, bravery and revenge. But that's probably enough for one night...Sleep well!

USELESS INFORMATION - ATTILA THE VIKING

Believe it or not, the king the Vikings called Atli in the saga of Sigurd and Gudrun has been identified as the terrible Attila the Hun, who beat up most of Asia.

46

THOR'S STORY

Thor was a bit of a hero to the Vikings. He was big and strong, with a magic belt that made him twice as big and strong if he pulled it tight. His magic hammer always hit the target, and came back to him when he'd thrown it.

One day Thor heard of a land of giants who were even bigger and stronger than him. Rising to the challenge this presented, he went in search of their land, with a servant and his friend Loki for company.

As it grew dark, they decided to break their journey. Thor spied a great hall in the forest and they decided to rest overnight. In the middle of their slumber, a great noise and shaking awoke them. They rushed into a smaller room, ready to protect themselves. But nothing further happened that night. As day broke, they were astounded to find the cause of the threat. A giant named Skrymir had been snoring at their side! The hall in which they had slept was his glove, and they had run into one of the fingers in fright. (*It's only a story, remember…*)

A SLEEPING GIANT

They followed the giant, who carried their loads and led the way. Eventually, they stopped to rest once more, and Skrymir fell fast asleep. Thor tried to get their food from his bundle, but the knots were too tight - even the mighty Thor could not untie them. He tried to wake Skrymir - he hit him and kicked him, and even whacked him one with his magic hammer. But Skrymir just brushed him away in his sleep, mumbling about the insects in the forest.

When Thor hit him again, Skrymir muttered once more about twigs dropping on him. Again Thor hit the giant, this time crashing the hammer down as hard as he could. The giant awoke sleepily: "An acorn has fallen on my head. Let's go."

Soon they reached the castle of the giant king. Skrymir warned Thor to be careful - he was just a piddly giant compared to the ones inside. The gates were locked, but (*as chance would have it*) Thor was small enough to crawl through a crack underneath them!

LOAD OF LOSERS

The king met them in the hall, and welcomed them to stay - but for one night only. "Unless," he said, "any of you is a champion…?"

The servant boy offered to race against someone - but even the old butler beat him easily. Loki's talent was for eating, so the king had a large trough of meat brought in. Loki ate and ate, and finished his half - but his giant opponent guzzled down the bones and the wooden trough too!

Thor decided to try his luck in a drinking contest (*typical Viking*). He was given a drinking horn, and told that most Vikings could finish it in one gulp. Thor drank and drank, but could hardly empty any of the liquid.
In his embarrassment, he offered to wrestle anybody who stepped forward. To his shame, the king's elderly old nurse pinned him to the ground.

FOOLED YA!

The king kept his promise, and let them stay one night only. As they left, the king made a confession. "Actually chaps, you were really too good to stay here any longer!"
"What?" cried Thor. "You're winding me up."
"I tricked you," confessed the king. "I was Skrymir, and I put a spell on my bundle to prevent you untying the knots. You nearly killed me, trying to wake me up!"

"My butler who ran so fast was, in fact, Thought. Nothing is faster than thought. Loki's opponent was Fire - and fire eats nearly as quickly as thought moves."

Thor looked amazed and confused (*know the feeling, mate*). "But what about the drinking contest?"

"Your drinking horn was dipped into the world's seas. All the oceans have fallen lower since you drank. And before you ask , the nurse you wrestled with was Old Age itself - and no-one can beat that."

Thor smiled with relief and regained pride. They left on good terms, with the giant king pleading for Thor never to come back!